I0440886

NEVER AGAIN!

Edward Carpenter

[ZHINGOORA BOOKS]

This edition is published by
Zhingoora Books.

Apart from any fair dealing for the purposes of research or private study, or criti-cism or review, this publication may only be reproduced, stored or transmitted, in any form or by any means, with the prior permission in writing of the publishers. All disputes are subject to exclusive jurisdiction of Mandsaur Courts only. For any suggestions and feedback or book on new concept/domain, please contact us at the email given below.

contact@Zhingoora.com

Never again must this Thing happen. The time has come — if the human race does not wish to destroy itself in its own madness — for men to make up their minds as to what they will do in the future; for now indeed is it true that we are come to the cross-roads, we stand at the Parting of the Ways.

The rapid and enormous growth of scientific invention makes it obvious that Violence ten times more potent and sinister than that which we are witnessing to-day may very shortly be available for our use — or abuse — in War. On the other hand who can doubt that the rapid growth of interchange and understanding among the peoples of the world is daily making Warfare itself, and the barbarities inevitably connected with it, more abhorrent to our common humanity?

Which of these lines are we to follow? Along which path are we to go? This is a question which the mass — peoples of Europe in the future — and not merely the Governments —- will have seriously to ponder and decide.

That bodies of men — as has happened a hundred times in the trenches in Northern France and even on the Eastern Front — should exchange morning salutations and songs in humorous amity, and then at a word of command should fall to shooting each other;

That peasants and artisans, and shopkeepers and students and schoolmasters, who have no quarrel whatever, who on the whole rather respect and honour each other, should with explosive bombs deliberately blow one another to bits so that even their own mothers could not recognize them; That human beings should use every devilish invention of science with the one purpose of maiming, blinding, destroying those against whom they have no personal grudge or grievance; All this is sheer madness.

Only a short time ago a private soldier said to me: "Yes, we had got to be such friends with those Bavarians in the trenches over against us that if we had returned there again I believe nothing could have made us fight with each other; but of course that point was perceived and we were moved to another part of the Line." What a criticism in a few words on the whole War! A hundred times this or something similar has happened, and a hundred and a thousand times these 'enemies' who have madly mutilated each other have — a few minutes later — been only too glad to dress each other's wounds and share the last contents of their water-bottles.

By all the heart-rending experiences which have now become so common and familiar to us;

By the fact that to-day there is hardly a family over the greater part of Europe that is not grieving bitterly over the loss of some dearest member of its circle;

By the white faces of the women clad in black, whom one sees everywhere in the streets of Berlin and Brussels and Paris and Vienna, of London and Milan and Belgrade and Petrograd;

By the sufferings of famine-stricken Poland, ravaged already three or four times in the last two years by opposing and alternate armies;

By the awful sufferings of the six or seven million Jews of the Russian Pale, hounded homeless in winter to and, fro over the frozen earth the old men and women and children perishing of exposure, fatigue, and starvation; By the agony of Serbia, and the despair of Belgium;

This must not be again!

By the five or six million actual combatants already slain; and, the strange spectacle of millions of Women (over half a million in Britain, more in France, multitudes in Germany and America) manufacturing man-destroying explosive shells in ceaseless stream by day and night; (And it is estimated that on the average some fifty shells are expended for every one man slain) By the terrified faces — as of drowning men — of those suffering in countless hospitals from shell-shock; by their trembling hands and, limbs and horrible dreams at night — pursued by an ever-living horror;

By the curses of the tender-hearted friend who collects in No-man's-land between the lines the scattered fragments of his comrade's body — the dabs of flesh, the hand, the head he knows so well, a boot with a foot still in it — and puts them all together in a sack for burial;

By the silent stupefaction of wives and mothers trying vainly to picture to themselves a death which cannot be pictured; by the insane laughter of those who having witnessed these things can no longer weep;

This must not be again!

By the beach at Gallipoli covered with the prostrate and writhing forms of men exhausted and emaciated with dysentery, who have crawled down from the hills only to lie out there in the terrible sun tormented with flies and thirst, or to shiver through the frosty night, waiting for the tardy arrival of the Hospital Ship;

By the hundreds of bodies thrown at the last into the sea at sunrise, for their unceremonious end;

And each poor body for all its loathsome state so loved, so loved by some one far away;

By the dear Lord who in the beautiful legend descended for three days into Hell that he might redeem mankind; but these have lived in an actual Hell for weeks and months together —

This must not be again!

By the growth and expansion of Science (God forgive the word!) which will inevitably make each future war more devilish and inhuman than the last;

By the cry of the black and coloured peoples of the Earth who have for long enough already said how hard and cruel the faces of the white men seemed to them, and who now think how black their souls are;

By the hardness of heart, the insensitiveness of a certain kind, which during a century or more now has been bred by the institutions of Commercialism;

By the habitual betrayal, through long periods of 'prosperity' and `peace,' of men by their fellows — of the weak by the powerful, of the generous by the mean, of the simple and thoughtless by the crafty and selfish;

By the huge dividends declared by Armament Firms; by the international agreements of these firms with one another, even to cozen their own respective Governments;

By the hundreds and hundreds of thousands of innocent folk trampled underfoot in the ditch of competition, the mad, race in which the devil takes the hindmost;

By the treacherous internal warfare of the ordinary industrial life of every country, the secret betrayal and murder of bodies and souls for profit — at last written out in letters of blood and fire across the continents, for all to behold —

This must not be again !

Let the Allies by all means accuse Germany of world-ambition and world-plunder, and let the German people accuse their Prussian lords but let every nation also search its own heart and accuse itself.

For have not the lords of every nation set before themselves the same goal, the goal of world-ambition and glory and 'empire' and plunder? And have not the mass-peoples of every nation stood meanly by and acclaimed the fraud, nor spoken out against it, silently consenting to these things in the prospect of some advantage also to themselves?

Have not all the nations without exception acted meanly and dastardly towards the out lying black races, and even towards those more civilized peoples whom they thought weaker than themselves — and now in the stress of war are they not finding that their own rights and liberties are being slowly filched from them?

Yes, that is, the end of Glory and of Greed.

But the day of glory is departed. The newspapers, it is true, still keep up the phrase. They talk of a battalion "covering itself with glory." But the men themselves do not talk so. They know too well what it all means. They see no glory in covering themselves with the blood of their brothers of the opposing trenches; with whom a few moments before they were joining in songs and jokes.

They only say: Now that we have begun, we will see it through — but it must not be Again.

Never I think in all the history of the world has there been a thing so great in its way as the present British Army and Navy. This enormous force, raised — except for a small remnant — by Voluntary enlistment from all classes of the nation, and inspired more by a general and protective sense towards the Motherland than by anything else, has fulfilled what it considered to be its duty and its honour with a devotion and a heroism unsurpassed. It were impossible to stay and recount its many wonderful deeds.

A young officer said to me one day — "Horrible as the whole thing is, yet it almost seems worth while, when you think of the splendid things done — and done too in such a simple matter-of-fact way: when you think of all the love and devotion poured out, and the lives our men have given one for the sake of another."

Great indeed is the spirit of such an army, great its magnanimity, its simplicity of mind, its unself-consciousness, its single concentration on its purpose.

Yet perhaps the most surprising thing about our men is that they have done all this with so little hatred in their hearts for the enemy.

Whatever the Germans may have felt, and whatever the French, the Britishers have just done their fighting in their own nonchalant way "because they had to" — with scarcely a shadow of malice or revenge — rather with that respect for a doughty opponent which always distinguishes the true fighter.

Think of that quaint story (Between The Lines, by Boyd Cable, pp 188 ff) of the German Burschen in their trenches, singing with pious enthusiasm the Song of Hate (probably commanded and compelled, poor devils, to sing it) and our men for days secretly listening, learning the words, practicing the tune on their muffled, mouth-organs; till having got it all complete they one morning, burst it forth in full chorus on the astonished Teutons, nor failed at the end to blaze out "Gott strafe England" at the top of, their voices as if they really meant it — and then subsided into a roar of laughter. They simply would not take the German "Hate" seriously.

Well, what can an enemy do with such an army? It would seem indeed to be invincible.

The other surprising thing about this Army is (but it is also in part true of the Russians and others) that the members of it not only bear so little malice in their heart of hearts against the enemy, but that all the time they (or nine-tenths of them) are giving their life-blood, for a Country which in hardly any available or adequate sense can really be said to belong to them.

Not one man of ours in ten, probably not one in a hundred, has any direct rights or interest in his native soil; and the Motherland has too often (at any rate in the past) turned out a stepmother who disowned him later when crippled in her service.

He is told that he is fighting for his country, but he finds that his real privilege is to die at the foot of a Trespass-board on some rich man's estate, singing bravely to the last that "Britons never, never shall be slaves!" He is told that he is defending his hearth and his home, and to prove that that is so, he is sent out on a far campaign to further some dubious scheme — in Mesopotamia! I think we cannot refuse to say that the good temper and they single-heartedness and the single mindedness of the British soldier are beyond all praise.

But, in another way, how admirable and how great has the French soldier proved himself to be!

The passion of Patriotism, the sheer love of their own country (in the case of the French, more truly "their own" than in the case of the British) has swept through France in a wave of devotion which consumed in its flame, one may almost say, the energies and the treasures of every household. To protect their beautiful land, their divine mistress, from violation by the German hordes was a thing for which all men — artists, literary men and all — were glad to die.

When at Meaux the French army (reorganized and reinforced) broke through the German centre and fell upon Von Kluck's left flank (his right being already threatened by the French Sixth Army), they were surely not men who fought, but spirits rather —

many of them almost ghosts, white with the fatigues and privations of a long retreat; but to save their beloved Paris they faced the enemy with a fury that nothing could resist.

A miracle was wrought (talk of Angels at Mons, it was Devils at Meaux), and Germany in that moment was defeated — even though it took two years more to make her acknowledge her defeat.

Think of Lieutenant Pericard who in a trench full of corpses at Bois-brule cried, suddenly entranced, in a loud voice, "Debout les morts!" and in a moment, as it were, the souls of their dead comrades were around his men, inspiring them to victory.

When again at Verdun week after week and month after month the French army endured tine almost hourly mass-attacks of the enemy battalions and the deluge of their shells (eight million shells, it is estimated the Germans threw in ten weeks), it still, though heavily punished, stood solid, and the whole of France stood solid behind it. France never doubted the conclusion; and the conclusion was never doubtful.

We have spoken of `glory,' but the day of ` la gloire ' has departed. France herself has ceased to speak of it — and there can be no better proof than that, of the change that has come over the minds of men .

France has emerged from the War a changed nation. The people who in 1870 made ribald verses and sang cynical songs over the plight of their country are now no more, and France emerges serious, resolute, to the great work which she has before her — of building the great first Democratic State of Europe and becoming the corner-stone of the future European Confederation.

And what shall we say of the German army? (In the moment and merely for the sake of brevity I leave the Belgians, Russians, Italians and Serbians aside.)

When I think of the great German army now scattered over Europe, fighting along that immense line (including the Austrian portion) of some 1,400 miles in extent; when I think of this on the whole so wonderfully goodhearted, genial, sociable people, these regiments of Westphalians, Wurtemburgers, Saxons, Bavarians, Hungarians, these men and boys from the fields and farms of Posen and Pomerania, the forests of Thuringia, the vineyards of the Rhine or the vegetable gardens of the Palatinate, these students from the Universities and scholars from the Technical Schools; plunged in this insane War, fighting in very truth for they know not what, and pouring out their life-blood, like water in obedience to the long-prepared schemes of their rulers — I am seized with an immense pity.

They have been told they are fighting to save their Fatherland. And as far as our argument is concerned it does not matter how falsely they have been instructed or what grain of actual truth there may be in the contention.

The point is that the vast majority of them believe this to be true; and they too, dear children, are giving their lives for their hearths and homes — they too are leading this hateful existence in trenches and mines, called to it by what seems to them a good conscience, and carried onward (in company with those they have left at home) in the mad millrace of public opinion.

However we may, blame the German High Command — and certainly we must blame those in power, who over such a long period deliberately prepared this war, and at the last so suddenly launched it upon Europe.

However we may blame the German High Command, we cannot refuse to acknowledge the really great qualities of their general Army: its extraordinary courage and devotion, its versatility and resource.

As to its goodheartedness, that is proved by the endless stories of spontaneous friendliness shown by the German troops even to their enemies, the individual rapprochements on occasions, the succour to the wounded, the Christmas songs and celebrations, and by the fact of advances of this kind so often coming first from the German side.

As to its good sense, that element certainly has not been wanting. Among the stories' above-mentioned as coming from the Front is one which I have every reason to believe is true. The Saxons one day, in their trenches thirty or forty yards away, put up a blackboard on which was written: "The English are fools!" The board was of course peppered with bullets, and went drown. Presently it reappeared with "The French are fools!" written on it. Being duly peppered again it went down, and came up with "The Russians are fools!" Same treatment. But when it, or a similar board, appeared for the fourth time, lo! the inscription was "The Austrians are fools!"; and when it appeared for the fifth time, "The Germans are fools!"; and the sixth time, "We are all fools!"

I don't think there could be much better sense than that.

And to think that the insane policy of a Government or Governments should bring about the wholesale slaughter of such mien as all these that I have described.

To think that the longer such a war goes on, the less heroic and generous it becomes, and the more dominated by hatred and revenge — by the wish to score a military victory or the desire to secure mere political and commercial advantages.

To think that nations who consider themselves civilized should be thus acting: so contrary to the natural laws and instincts of humanity that often in order for a bayonet charge men must be primed with liquor to the verge of intoxication .

We need not go further.

Of the three great nations primarily involved those indeed of which we can speak most confidently, knowing them best — it is intolerable to think they should thus mutilate and destroy each other.

All we can say is: Never again must this thing happen!

When one thinks of the whole dread Coil and Entanglement, and, what it is for, the mind reels in despair.

When one thinks of the marvellous scientific ingenuity and skill, directed in a kind of diabolic concentration on the one purpose of slaughter.

Of the huge guns, the 12.5's, weighing 40 tons apiece, and boxed and rifled to the nicety of the thousandth part of an inch (I have watched them being made at Sheffield).

Of the larger 15 in. guns, with range of 13 or 14 miles, so accurate that the shells thrown at that distance will deviate hardly a couple of yards to the right hand or the left of their line of fire (and in the Jutland battle the firing opened at nearly 11 miles).

Of the still larger guns even now being constructed.

Of the shells themselves varying from a few pounds to nearly, a ton in weight, and so delicately fashioned that the moment of their explosion can be positively timed to the tenth part of a second:

When one thinks of the ingenuity put into aeroplanes and airships, and almost entirely with a view to the destruction of life;

Of the automatic steering of submarine torpedoes by means of gyroscopes, so that when deviated by any obstacle or accident from their set course they will actually return of themselves to that course again;

Of the everlasting duel going on in any one country between armour plates and projectiles but of course always between the armour plates of one firm and the projectiles of another (since obviously for any one firm to prove its own inferiority in either line would be bad business)!

Of the competition even now in progress between the Russian universities for the invention of a new explosive or a new gas more devastating than any hitherto produced;

Of the weighty Advisory Committee of scientific Experts sitting permanently in Britain for the discussion and handling of the technical problems of the War;

When one thinks of what a Paradise all this ingenuity, all this expenditure of labour and treasure, might make of our mortal Earth — if it were only decently employed;

That Great Britain alone has already spent on the War enough to provide every family in the whole kingdom with a comfortable cottage and an acre of land;

When further one thinks of all the mass of human material there is, such as we have already described — of the very finest quality, and fit to build the most splendid races and cities "the sun ever shone upon" — and then that it is being used for these utterly senseless purposes;

How heart-rending the waste and the folly! How disgusting the sin of those who are responsible!

But to-day surely the armies themselves of these three countries are beginning to see through the illusions which have been dangled before then so long by those in power — the "My-country — right-or-wrong" kind of Patriotism which has so often been evoked only in order to serve the plots of private schemers;

They are surely beginning to see that the directing of State-policy and foreign relations must no longer be left in the hands of a few highborn diplomats (mostly ignorant of the actual modern world amid which they live), but must be subject to the severest scrutiny and surveillance by the people at large and their representatives;

They are beginning to see that if courage, devotion to an Idea, love of the Father- or Mother-land, Fidelity of comrade to comrade, Efficiency, daring in Adventure, exactness in Organization, and so forth, are the qualities which in the past have made the profession of arms great and glorious, it is these very qualities which will be demanded and evoked for all future time in the great free armies of Industry.

For with the cessation of Militarism as the leading principle of national life must inevitably come the liberation of Industry — else the last state of our societies will indeed be worse than the first.

Truly there is nothing very exhilarating about Industry as it has in modern times been conceived, and one does not altogether wonder that all down the centuries the man with the sword has despised the man with the hoe, since the latter has generally been little better than a slave.

But when once Labour is freed — or rather when once it frees itself — from the thraldom, of the old Feudal system, and finally from the fearful burden of modern Capitalism — when once it can lift its head and see the great constructive vision of the new society which awaits it — then surely it will perceive that all the great qualities we have named as exhibited in the past in the old destructive Warfare, and now become the splendid heritage of the peoples of Europe, will be necessary and will have a field for their exercise in the beneficent constructive conquests of Nature and the building up on Earth of that great City of the Sun which for so many ages has been the dream and inspiration of Man.

And of the old mad Warfare it will then say This odious and inhuman Thing must never be again!

In conclusion, and to look to the future:

I think we may see that the new conception of life will only come through the peeling off in the various nations of the old husks of the diplomatic, military, legal, and commercial classes, with their antiquated, narrow-minded and profoundly. irreligious and inhuman standards — those husks which have so long restricted and strangulated the growing life within.

It will only come with the determination of the workers (that is, of everybody) to produce things useful, profitable, and beautiful, in free and rational co-operation — things useful because deliberately made for use, things profitable for all because not made for the gain of the few, and things beautiful because of the joy and gladness wrought into their very production.

Simultaneously with this peeling off, of the Old, and disclosure of the New, will of necessity appear — indeed it is taking shape already the blossom of international solidarity and federation — the common cause of Humanity and of Labour liberated over the world.

Naturally such process will not mature all at once. It may, bit that the four Western nations, England, France, Italy and Belgium, combining with some of the neutral States, will constitute the first European Federationor at any rate the nucleus of a Federation destined, as it expands to absorb within its borders Germany herself (of course when she shall have taken on her true republican form) and the other States in due succession.

Such Federation when firmly consolidated might, it is not unlikely, still retain for a long period a military system, of some kind, if only for its own protection against outlying and non European dangers; but that military system would be small and secondary. It right reasonably be no more dominant or meddlesome than the military system of China has been during the last thousand years in comparison with the massive imperturbability of the great Chinese Empire itself.

Meanwhile let us remember how important it is for the future of the world that each nation and people should be free to contribute its special quality and character to the whole; nor be ridden-over roughshod by the others;

That each should contribute, in Trade or otherwise, its special gifts or facilities; and that the Internationalism which already rules in labour affairs and in Commerce and Science and Fashion and Finance and Philanthropy and Literature and Art and Music, should at last be recognized in Politics.

Let us further remember how important it is that every man and woman should insist on the rights of Personality to preserve sacred his or her most intimate sense of selfness and duty the very, essence of Freedom.

Though I do not, for instance, think that a refusal to fight under any condition or circumstance can reasonably be maintained to its logical conclusion, and though I certainly would not engage myself to refuse to fight in any and every case. Still, I do honour and respect the genuine conscientious objectors (of whom there are great numbers) very sincerely.

Some of them may, be narrow-minded and faddist (as conscience often is), but let us remember that the great things of History have been initiated by such folk.

It was they who barred and broke the gladiatorial games at Rome; it was they, who, steered the "Mayflower" across the Atlantic, and started the great Republic of the United States;

And it is they, who are possibly sowing the seed a great Movement which will spread all over Europe, and ultimately by opposing compulsory military service inaugurate a world-era of Peace. (For certainly, without Conscription the Continental Powers would never have become involved in the present war)

Let us recognize the right and the duty of each man to ponder these world-problems for himself: to play his part and to make his own voice heard in the solution of them.

Let us recognize the falsity of Science divorced from the Heart, and begin to-day to create a political, an economic, and a material world which shall be the true and satisfying expression of the real human soul;

Let us acknowledge even at the last that the War may have been a, necessary evil to show us by contrast the way, of deliverance;

Let us render, homage to those who have given their lives in it; let us vow that their great sacrifice shall not be in vain, but shall consecrate for us a new purpose and a new ideal;

Let us believe that Love, not Hatred, is the power by which in the end the World will be saved;

And let us pray that a Heroism equal to that, shown to-day in the cause of Destruction may urge us in the future towards a great and glorious Constructive era in social life — and inspire us with a new hope:

Out of purgatory to build a paradise, in which the ugliness, vulgarity, sordidness and cruelty of the present scheme of things will be repeated.

August 1916

End of the book.

www.ingramcontent.com/pod-product-compliance
Lightning Source LLC
Chambersburg PA
CBHW071349310526
45730CB00018B/1397